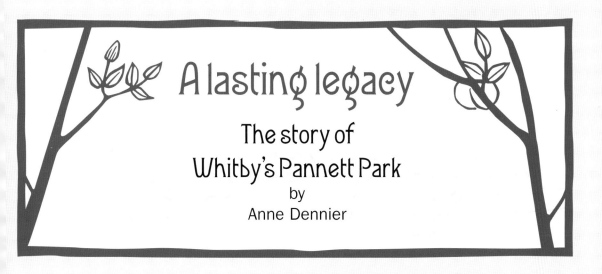

A lasting legacy

The story of Whitby's Pannett Park

by
Anne Dennier

WHITBY
LITERARY &
PHILOSOPHICAL
SOCIETY

Anne Dennier is a town planner by profession and lectured at the University of Liverpool for much of her career. The conservation of both the built and natural environment has always been a particular interest. She retired to Sleights about fourteen years ago and, as a voluntary assistant in the Whitby Literary and Philosophical Society Library at the Museum, became aware of the deteriorating state of Pannett Park. Having joined the Friends she, with Beverley Brown, contributed a survey of the Park's trees and shrubs to the matching funding for a bid to the Heritage Lottery Fund. Later, she volunteered to research and write the history of the Park.

Published by Whitby Literary & Philosophical Society, 2009.

ISBN 978-0-902074-19-4

Printed by Billingham Press Ltd.

Acknowledgements

I wish to say, first, how much I appreciate the co-operation of Parry Thornton, without whose meticulous researches in the Whitby Gazette, I could not have written this book. The Whitby Gazette was, indeed, a primary source of information on the history of the Park and I thank the Editor for his permission to quote from it. I am also most grateful for the support and patience of my colleagues and friends in the Whitby Literary and Philosophical Society, especially those in the Library. Too numerous to mention individually, I hope they will all accept my assurance that their help in finding material and illustrations was invaluable. Caroline Stanford kindly provided material on William Collier, her grandfather, which would not otherwise have come to light. I also thank my friends Brenda McLean and Niall Carson for their help with my drafts.

The Parks for People grant awarded to Pannett Park provided for the publication of this book. Robert Everiss, the Park Project Officer, has given me cheerful encouragement and kept me in touch with others involved in the Project including the Friends of Pannett Park, TGP Landscape Architects and Fiona Green, whose research into the making of the Park was most useful. Lastly I should like to thank Marcus Byron for his designs and unfailing patience.

Picture Credits

A lasting legacy

The story of Whitby's Pannett Park

by Anne Dennier

Contents

Above:

Whitby in the age
of coal

Introduction

Gardens and open spaces have been treasured wherever towns have grown too large for people to escape easily from crowded streets to enjoy fresh air in their leisure time.

By the late 18th century people of fashion wanted, and were willing to pay for, 'pleasure grounds' where they could enjoy gardens with pretty walks, shady trees, lawns and flowers and, perhaps, some entertainment. Such gardens were soon associated with health and spa waters, however disgusting they tasted, were often one of the attractions. Spas were considered essential in the new resorts and sea-side towns which sprang up. Scarborough was one of the first of these and Whitby followed later.

Meanwhile, as industrial towns and cities grew during the 19th century, more and more people had nowhere to go for fresh air and exercise. Sometimes land was given for public use – the Royal Parks in London are a fine example; sometimes ancient commons were preserved. But the idea of creating public parks, free to all, was a Victorian innovation. It sprang from the realisation that everyone needed access to green, open spaces for the sake of their own health and the well-being of the community.

However, there were problems in providing public parks. The first was the capital cost of acquiring a site and laying it out; the second was the on-going cost of maintaining it. The land might be given by a local benefactor who might also lay out the park before it was handed over, or the local authority might undertake some or all of the initial expense. But in either case the upkeep of the park would be a charge on the community. The political issues which cropped up in meeting these expenses could take many years to resolve.

This book tells the story of how Whitby, eventually, came to have its own public park, Pannett Park.

VICTORIA SPA

Bagdale

- Whitby

Chapter 1.
The first idea

The idea of creating a park in Whitby first came up in the 1830s. The town was crowded into the narrow Esk valley. The roads into it were steep and the streets narrow and hazardous for local people and visitors alike.

An Act of Parliament in 1837 granted powers to build a new road to link Bagdale and Flowergate Cross, the route that is now Chubb Hill Road, and to buy enough land at the same time to make a park above Bagdale. This open land, known as the Chubb Hill Estate, belonged to Henry Walker Yeoman, Archdeacon of Cleveland. However the scheme came to nothing. Money was needed for other urgent improvements in the town. Shortly afterwards George Hudson brought the first railway to come into Whitby from Pickering. Thinking to encourage visitors who might come for the healthy sea-side air and the spa waters, he also began to develop property on the West Cliff and built the road we know today as the Khyber Pass from the harbour-side to the cliff top.

The success of Hudson's scheme did indeed bring more visitors to Whitby. Prints of the town's attractions at the time show bathing huts on the beach and elegant people walking on the West Pier and the cliff paths. As time went on there were those who argued that to attract more visitors, and encourage them to stay longer, the town needed some pleasant, sheltered place to walk. The cliffs and the beach could be too exposed to the blasts of the north-east winds for comfort. A park would be invaluable. At the same time another route up to West Cliff was needed. A broad, tree-lined carriageway would impress visitors and double as a promenade. Queen Victoria's Golden Jubilee was to be celebrated in 1887. What better way to mark this great event than to build such a road and a park too?

Right:

George Hudson
c1800 -1871

Project Gutenberg

Far right:

Announcement of early Whitby and Pickering Railway services in the Yorkshire Gazette.

Courtesy Yorkshire Gazette

CHEAP, SAFE, & EXPEDITIOUS TRAVELLING.
WHITBY & PICKERING RAILWAY
THE Public are respectfully informed that the RAILWAY COACHES, during the SUMMER MONTHS, will start from Whitby and Pickering, at the following Hours, viz.—
From WHITBY to PICKERING, every Morning at 7 o'Clock, and every Evening, at 5 o'Clock.
From PICKERING to WHITBY, every Morning at Half-past 8 o'Clock and every Evening, after the arrival of the York Coach (about Half-past 5 o'Clock).
(Sundays excepted.)
FARES.—INSIDE, 3s. 6d.—CAB, 3s.—TOP, 2s. 6d.
N. B. No Gratuity allowed to be taken by Guard, Coachman, Porter, or other Servant of the Company.
PASSENGERS may be Booked at York, at the BLACK SWAN and TAVERN COACH OFFICES, to proceed to Whitby by the NEPTUNE COACH, which leaves York every Day, (Sundays excepted) at 2 o'Clock in the Afternoon; and Passengers leaving Whitby by the 7 o'Clock Coach will be forwarded to York to arrive in time for the Coaches proceeding to Sheffield, Hull, Leeds Manchester, Liverpool, and London.
Trucks and Cribs for the conveyance of Carriages and Horses may be had on notice.

Taking the air on
the West Pier
Rock's Royal Cabinet,
Album of Whitby, Rock & Co.

Chubb Hill Estate
(site of the park)

Whitby in 1841
Francis Pickernell

Archdeacon Yeoman's land had not been built on and was used for orchards, market gardens and a small dairy farm. Could he be persuaded to part with it? Negotiations were opened by the Local District Board which was responsible for such improvements. The Archdeacon began the bidding at £20,000 but was persuaded to come down to £15,000 – this for about 10 acres (4 ha), plainly a building land valuation. The Board's Valuer, no doubt thinking that much of the site was rather too steep for housing, said about £9,500 would be a reasonable price. The Archdeacon would not budge but was eventually persuaded to sell 1.12 acres (0.48 ha) - just enough land for a carriage road 60' (20m) wide. It was to have a mini-circus half way up the hill and trees on either side so it would serve the planned dual purpose. Even so it seemed expensive to some in authority and the Board would not have gone ahead without a contribution of £800 from their clerk, none other than Robert Elliott Pannett. The idea of creating a park at the same time was unfortunately abandoned on grounds of expense and the continuing need for public works elsewhere in the town.

Above:

Archdeacon HW Yeoman

Left:

The Chubb Hill Estate in 1866 seen from Downdinner Hill near the junction with Bagdale. The houses in St Hilda's Terrace stand on the horizon.

On November 24th 1886, with some ceremony, the first sod was cut for the road. Unfortunately there were problems. It is not clear whether these were due to changes in the exact route and the design or to unexpected construction problems. Whatever the cause, the road was not completed until the winter of 1897/98. By this time the Whitby Urban District Council, created in 1894, was in charge and Mr Pannett was no longer involved. He was devoting his energies to the North Riding of Yorkshire County Council.

Below:

Work starts on Chubb Hill Road

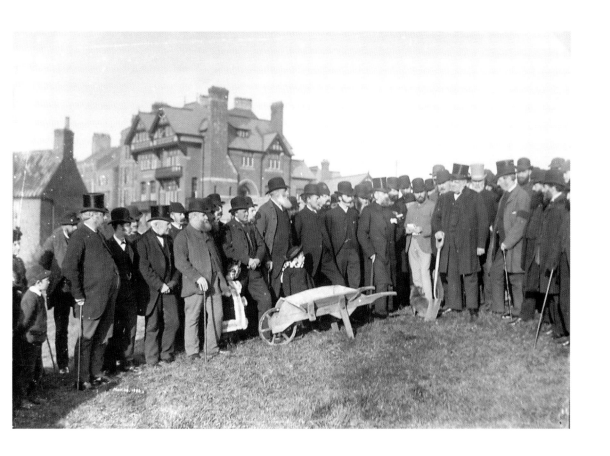

Chapter 2.
Robert Elliot Pannett (1834 - 1920)

Robert Elliott Pannett's father, William Pannett, came from Sussex to the north as the servant of a wealthy Whitby man. In 1823 he married a local girl, Alice Elliott, and set up shop on St Ann's Staith as a hairdresser, perfumier and *'manufacturer of ornamental hair'*. They had two children, first Sarah then Robert Elliott who was born in 1834.

Robert was evidently a clever boy. He went to school at Mr Gibson's Bagdale Academy, until he was twelve. When he left school he was taken on by a Whitby solicitor who later assigned his articles to the firm of Bell, Broderick and Gray in London where he lived for a number of years. He was admitted solicitor in November 1858 and returned to Whitby to begin a life-long partnership with Matthew Gray's family firm in Flowergate. Sadly, William Pannett had died a few months before his son's return; his wife kept on the hairdressing business for several years.

Above:

Mr Pannett as a young man

Left:

Silhouette of Robert Elliot Pannett, aged 10

We know little of Robert Elliott Pannett's private life. The censuses show that he lived with his mother and sister in St Ann's Staith by the harbour until they moved up to 14 Normanby Terrace in the late 1860s where he remained for the rest of his life. Both his mother and his sister (who like himself never married) died in the 1870s. Mr Pannett employed a housekeeper and evidently looked after his servants well for they stayed with him for many years and were remembered in his will. He seems to have made long-standing friendships and visited his Sussex relations in Brighton when he lived in London. He left bequests to many friends though he seems to have lost touch with most of his relations since he mentions only one but left money for any others who might be traced. It was said that he spoke more than one foreign language and he certainly took a great interest in the arts for he collected paintings (especially those of his contemporary George Weatherill), as well as books, silver and other treasures.

Above:

An untitled painting showing Whitby harbour by George Weatherill

Mr Pannett came of dissenting stock and was a staunch Methodist, closely involved in the Brunswick Street Church and with its Sunday School. Towards the end of his life it seems that he moved in a tight circle of friends, mostly people with whom he shared his professional and public life as well as his faith. Judging by his involvement in charities, such as those for the blind, and by reports of kindly help quietly given to people in need, he was a benevolent and thoughtful man.

Left:
Mr Pannett in 1892

Below:
Brunswick Methodist
Church

Throughout his long life Mr Pannett had three abiding objectives: to improve and enhance Whitby as a town for both local people and visitors; to promote education especially in the arts and literature; and to support the Methodist Church.

Involvement in local government was a way of achieving the first two of these objectives. He was appointed Clerk to the Town Improvement Commission in 1866 and served them and their successors, the District Local Board. In 1888, he became a founder member of the North Riding County Council representing Whitby West Ward. There he served on various committees including Education, and Agriculture and Fisheries. He also took a great interest in the management of Whitby Harbour. In 1908 he was elected an Alderman of the County Council, a prized honour seldom bestowed these days. He also acted as a magistrate from 1903.

Among his many interests, education was possibly the most important to him. He was instrumental in persuading the County Council to fund the County School (later the Grammar School and now the Community College) and was Chairman of its Board of Governors from its opening in 1912 until 1915. He promoted the teaching of science to a high standard by insisting on really good equipment and

financed the Pannett Art School which was used by the wider public as well as the pupils. He had a great deal to do with the success of the grand, ceremonial opening of the school in 1912; it may have been one of his proudest moments. However, he was also generous in supporting other improvements in Whitby. For example, he paid for lighting on the West Pier, always a popular promenade, and for better access to the Wesleyan Church above Church Street (now demolished) as well as contributing to the development of the Brunswick Church and its new school room to which he donated some 300 books.

Alderman Pannett evidently invested his money wisely for in his will, apart from personal bequests, he left land for a garden for the Seamen's Hospital in Church Street; land for a children's playground in Fylingthorpe; money and property to build an organ at the Brunswick School Room and money for the art room at the County School. Above all, he bequeathed, in a Trust, the Chubb Hill Estate and the money to make a park and build an art gallery there which were to be open and free to Whitby citizens for all time. His paintings, treasures and books were to be on view in this art gallery except for one particularly precious piece of medieval embroidery which he willed to the Victoria and Albert Museum.

The story of how this benevolent gentleman came to own the Chubb Hill Estate and why he wanted it to be made into a park is the subject of the next chapter.

Above:

Alderman Pannett handing the key to the County School to the Duchess of Albany at the opening ceremony in 1912
Courtesy of Whitby Community College

Left:

The Chubb Hill Estate in 1866 seen from Downdinner Hill near the junction with Bagdale. The houses in St Hilda's Terrace can be seen on the horizon

Chapter 3.
The park takes shape

I n May 1891 the Whitby Gazette reported that the Chubb Hill Estate, Archdeacon Yeoman's land, was on the market. The Editor thought it *'eminently desirable that it is not built on'* but the only hope was that *'a public spirited man-of-means will buy it and make a present of it to the town'*.

However, nothing happened. Mr Pannett's opportunity to demonstrate his public spirit came later when he bought the Estate in 1902. He paid £8600 for a little more than eight acres (some 3.2 ha). At about the same time he bought the Victoria Spa Well House for £41. The old spa had been re-housed in a new building when Broomfield Terrace was built in Bagdale opposite the Estate. People still drank the iron-rich waters.

The market gardens and nurseries with their fruit trees on the Chubb Hill Estate continued in business while Alderman Pannett tried to persuade the Urban District Council to take the land as a gift and make a park. The Council however, was very wary of the expense. While some agreed that it would benefit Whitby people and visitors would enjoy it, others considered a park a great waste of money and unlikely to extend the season. Letters in the Gazette argued that the bracing beach was all that Whitby needed and a cliff lift would be more use to visitors; or that the expense would add so much to the rates that visitors who had liked Whitby well enough to buy houses here would leave the town.

Above:
The Victoria Spa Well House can be found behind Broomfield Terrace. Whitby Civic Society occasionally open it to the public
Drawing by Anne Dennier

Right, top:
St Hilda's Terrace before the road was widened

Right, below:
Map of Chubb Hill Estate and environs OS 1913.
Ordnance Survey

widen St Hilda's Terrace and lay out the estate with such choice and ambitious amenities as tennis courts, croquet lawns, bowling greens, pavilions, maybe a concert hall, and a winter garden! But Councillor Harmston, who was reported as being sympathetic to the idea of a park, probably voiced the mood of the Council when he said – *'a large scheme like this requires a great deal of careful thought'*. So much thought, indeed, that nothing happened.

Time rolled on until in July 1920 Robert Elliott Pannett, now 86 years old, died. Determined to the end to achieve his objective, he bequeathed the Chubb Hill Estate and the Spa Well House to the people of Whitby with the intention that, after a little land was taken to widen St. Hilda's Terrace, a park should be laid out and an art gallery/museum built in it to house his pictures, books and other collections. He set up a trust with four trustees to manage the process and left assets to accomplish his plans and secure the future of the Park and Gallery.

Patience was the order of the day. Negotiations reached a peak through the spring and summer of 1913. Alderman Pannett was determined that access to the park should be free for all. He also argued for a long-standing proposal to add to the elegance of St Hilda's Terrace by widening the road to 60' (20m) from the junction with Chubb Hill Road to Union Road. The Council got as far as considering a Provisional Order which would allow them to acquire the Spa,

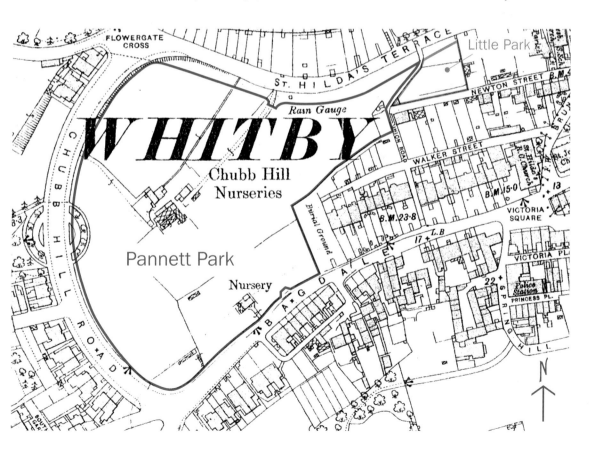

The Trustees

The four trustees were appointed from among Alderman Pannett's close and valued friends. The senior member was Mr Thomas Warters whose experience was mainly in accountancy. The others were Mr R W White, a Partner in the Alderman's old firm of solicitors; Mr George Thompson, an auctioneer in the town; and Miss Annie P Robinson, the Alderman's housekeeper. Unfortunately, especially for Mr Warters on whom the burden of carrying out his old friend's wishes increasingly fell, Miss Robinson died in 1921, and both Mr Thompson and Mr White died a few years later. A colleague of Mr White's, Mr Vivian Seaton Gray, took over from him and, with Mr Warters, saw the business completed.

The trustees had many tasks to carry out since the Alderman had left money and assets to other good causes as well as to friends. It took time to settle matters such as taxes. Unfortunately the value of the assets and property in their care fell as events such as the General Strike of 1926 and the Stock Market crash of 1929 were accompanied by severe economic depression. Mr Warters repeatedly emphasised that there was less money available for the park and the art gallery than either the Alderman or his trustees had anticipated.

Getting started

The first task was to gain possession of the land. It had been the Alderman's specific wish that the tenants should have time to find alternative premises. The nursery adjoining St. Hilda's Terrace, run by Messrs Williamson and Wood, had most difficulty in coming to an agreement and they did not leave until 1924. This was a key property since it contained the only substantial area of level ground. Its access is preserved in the main entrance to the park from St. Hilda's Terrace and the house and working area were roughly where the art gallery now stands. St Hilda's Terrace was widened in 1921, thanks to a financial contribution from Mr Warters.

Above:
Mr Vivian Seaton Gray
with his dog, Peggy

Left:
Thomas Warters Esq.
Portrait in oils by
Ernest Moore

Right, in box:
William Collier (on
the left) with his
brother and a colleague
© Ord Family

Above:
St Hilda's Terrace
widened - the wall was
built with re-used stone

Right:
The gate to the cottage
above Bagdale

The cottage above Bagdale, famously photographed
by Frank Meadow Sutcliffe, was retained but needed
a great deal of improvement. It became the home of
Mr William Collier, the first Park Keeper.

William Collier (1893 – 1977)

William Collier went to work with his father, who was
a gardener employed by the Urban District Council,
when he was nineteen. He was conscripted in 1915
and served in France with the Royal Engineers during
the 1914-18 War, rejoining his father when he was
de-mobbed. When work on the Chubb Hill Estate first
started both he and his father were involved but it
was William who, appointed Supervisor of the Park,
was responsible for seeing that the Trustees' and the
designer's (Mr Brydon's) wishes were carried out. In
1929 the Whitby Gazette reported that *'he thoroughly
deserves the many compliments paid him for the care
and attention he devotes to his duties and which is
reflected in the magnificent display of flowers and
their delightful arrangement'*. Mr Warters thanked him
publicly when the park was handed over to the Urban
District Council and later wrote that *'Mr Brydon, on
several occasions complimented the Trustees on
having such an able person as William Collier to look
after their interests'*.

In 1933 he married Edith Stephenson in the
Brunswick Methodist Church. They moved into the
Bagdale Cottage where they lived with their daughter,
Myra, until he retired in 1959. He looked after the
visitors to the park and always took great pride in its
upkeep. He was also in much demand as a judge of
flowers and vegetables at local horticultural shows.

The Trustees' choices

The trustees had to choose designers, architects and contractors for both the park and the art gallery. Kent and Brydon, well-known landscape designers and nurserymen of Darlington, were engaged to design the park. In practice it was Mr Walter Brydon who took on the task. It seems that he suggested the architects Hays and Gray of Wingate in Co. Durham might design the art gallery and, following a competition (arbitrated by Mr F Tugwell of Scarborough), they were appointed. The firm of Charles Hebditch of Loftus was contracted to build it.

Matters became more complicated when the Rev the Marquis of Normanby, Patron of the Whitby Literary and Philosophical Society, proposed that they should build a museum behind the art gallery. The Society was founded in 1823 and had amassed a large collection ranging through archaeology and everything to do with Whitby Abbey, geology and the Jurassic fossils, the jet industry, shipping, ship building and much else to do with life in the Whitby area. The museum had premises on Pier Road which were seriously over-crowded by the 1920s. (The Quayside Restaurant now occupies the building.) Everyone agreed that moving the museum up to the park would be a good idea. The Society's collections would be much better displayed and some of Alderman Pannett's items and his books could be more suitably housed with the museum's treasures. All this would add to the attractions of the park.

However, the trustees found there were management and legal problems to overcome. The Alderman had insisted on free access for the people of Whitby but the Society needed the income from admissions to finance their museum. There were questions of responsibility for upkeep and maintenance of the buildings and other issues concerning the Trust's obligations which could only be settled in the High Court. The Judge approved the ideas put forward but could not issue an order until all the building plans were submitted. The Society could not raise quite enough money to go ahead but the architects were asked to design the art gallery bearing in mind the prospect of adding the museum later.

The first important event

The foundation stone of the art gallery was laid on Wednesday, 9th March 1927 by Lord Normanby. Wednesday was chosen so that as many Whitby people as possible could come to see it – all the shops closed on Wednesday afternoon at that time. Lord Normanby and his family sat on a temporary platform with several civic dignitaries and many people gathered round, some seated on benches, some standing. All were well wrapped up but they probably felt cold by the time the speeches were over! Mr Warters, in particular, spoke at length to explain why it had taken seven years to get to this stage. Work had already started on the park and people were able to walk about the grounds after the ceremony.

A year later the art gallery was finished and the park sufficiently advanced for it to be opened officially. On August 1st, again a Wednesday afternoon and fortunately sunny, hundreds of people assembled to witness Sir Hugh Bell, Lord Lieutenant of the County, declare both open. Many of the same dignitaries gathered on the steps of the art gallery and again many speeches followed. Tributes were paid to the generosity of both Alderman Pannett and the people who had donated in money and in kind to both the art collection and the park. Mr Warters warned again that the Trust's assets were depreciating but he still hoped that when they handed over to the Council there would be some money to help with maintenance. The event was reported at length in the Whitby Gazette.

OPENING
— OF —

PANNETT PARK & ART GALLERY

BY

THE LORD-LIEUTENANT OF THE
NORTH RIDING OF YORKSHIRE

Sir Hugh Bell, Bart., C.B.

The Most Hon. and Rev. the Marquis of Normanby

PRESIDING

ON THE AFTERNOON OF

1ST AUGUST, 1928

AT 2.45 P.M.

Admission to Gallery up to 6 o'clock, 1/- each
From 6 to 8 p.m., 6d. each

Price, 3d. each.

Far left:

The Rev. the 3rd Marquis of Normanby. Portrait in oils (1928) by Donald Wood

Left:

The Architect's design for the Art Gallery

Above:

The leaflet written by Frank Meadow Sutcliffe on the opening of the Art Gallery

Left:

Mr Thomas Warters addressing the company at the ceremony for the laying of the foundation stone for the Art Gallery

Below:

Crowds at the opening ceremony for the completed Art Gallery

The several contributors

Many local people contributed to the park but two families were particularly important: those of Captain Kirby and Mr Warters.

Captain Kirby lived opposite the park in Chubb Hill Road and expressed a wish to contribute something to the scheme which the Trust could not well afford. Unfortunately he died before anything was settled but his wife and daughters decided to donate the lily pool and the shelter, which stood above it, in his memory. These were designed by Mr Brydon and built at a cost of nearly £800. At that time it was hoped to pipe in water from the Spa Well House, which accounts for the basin built into the back wall of the shelter. This, however, was never done; possibly the engineering problems of bringing the water from the other side of Bagdale were too formidable or the cost was too high.

Mr Warters, as mentioned earlier, provided funds, to the tune of £1400, to complete the widening of St Hilda's Terrace by taking out a mortgage to defray the cost. In 1928 he bought a large garden on the corner of Union Road and St Hilda's Terrace, *'stocked with fruit trees, a greenhouse and a vinery'* which he added to the park. We know it as the Little Park. Mrs Warters gave seats, as many as 38 in the first instance and possibly more later. Other people gave seats too. Unfortunately none have survived.

Several people donated money for plants. Some, like Judge Chapman and W A Headlam, favoured specimen trees; others, Sir John Harrowing, Mr F H Pyman and Mr W O Turnbull for example, liked rhododendrons and other shrubs. Mr Walter Pyman and Mr Brydon himself were evidently rockery enthusiasts. Mr Pyman's contribution provided the plants for a substantial display beside Chubb Hill Road; Mr Brydon gave those for the rockery beside Union Road.

Left:
Captain Kirby and his family outside their house

Above:
Lily pool

Two donors shared Alderman Pannett's interest in caged birds, a popular hobby at the time. Public parks often included an aviary and in May 1930, Miss Coble, who lived nearby in Bagdale, donated one with 50 birds. A little later, Mr T Grainger of Skelton added more. This aviary stood at the side of the lily pool shelter.

One other contribution is worth mentioning. Whalebone arches were once a common sight in the area. An old shed by the River Esk which was supported by seven pairs of whale jaw-bones was being taken down. Two pairs, each about 17' (6m) high, were sent up to Pannett Park and one of them was erected on a path near St. Hilda's Terrace. The site of the second arch is not recorded.

Top left:
Watching goldfish in the lily pool
Tindale Collection

Top right:
The whalebone arch in winter

Left:
The basin built in anticipation of delivering spa water into the park

Above:
Little Park in 2008

The museum is built

Fortunately the Literary and Philosophical Society soon raised the money to build their new museum to Hays and Gray's design and it was opened in 1931 by Lord Harewood. At that time there was only the central room, 64' (19.5 m) square, which is still the core exhibition space, with a small curator's office and a workshop attached on either side and an entrance lobby facing Chubb Hill Road. This is now the way in from the car park.

Above:

The Rockery near Chubb Hill Road. The photograph is undated but must have been taken soon after the plants were established
Courtesy of the Ord family

Top:

The museum was built and in use though the park was not finished

The Trust is wound up, its task completed

By 1932 the Trust had done its work. The High Court was satisfied with all the arrangements which had been agreed. The art gallery was up and running, the park was laid out except for the north-west corner between the museum and St Hilda's Terrace. The Trust could be wound up, no doubt to the great relief of Mr Warters and Mr Seaton Gray.

The death of the Rev the Marquis of Normanby delayed the ceremony until November. Mr Warters was by then too weak to attend and Mr Seaton Gray read his speech for him. Various deeds and a list of the donors were handed over to Whitby Urban District Council and the Honorary Curator of the Museum, Mr H P Kendall, presented a ceremonial peppercorn symbolic of the rent for the building. The Chairman of the Council, Councillor M Simpson, accepted on their behalf responsibility for the art gallery and the park which were 'to be kept for the people of Whitby for ever'. The few – very few – remaining assets were also handed over in the hope that they would help cover some of the maintenance costs.

SPRING IN PANNETT PARK, WHITBY

Above:

The park in spring

WHITBY GAZETTE

WHITBY'S JUBILEE GATES

Mrs. Turton, Major R. B. Turton, Miss Mavis Sawdon, Mrs. Sinclair, Councillor W. H. Sinclair, and Mr. Britten (the Parks Superintendent) entering Pannett Park after the gates had been opened by Mrs. Sinclair

The last corner of the park is finished

Mr Warters had hoped for a government grant to help with the cost of dealing with the unfinished north-west corner of the park but none was forthcoming. In 1935, the Whitby Gazette reported that, at last, it was being laid out under the supervision of Mr Britten, the Parks Superintendent. Trees had been planted and this *'eyesore is already taking on an attractive appearance'*. Lawns and paths were planned. A few weeks later it transpired that there was to be a new entrance at the junction of St Hilda's Terrace and Chubb Hill Road which would prove convenient to the *'largely increased number of residents in the Upgang direction'*.

The Council had decided to order a handsome iron gate for this entrance to mark King George V's twenty five years on the throne. Still known as the Jubilee Gate, it was made by a group of unemployed miners in Guisborough who, four years earlier had, with the help of the local Social Service Movement, set about learning to fashion ornamental ironwork. Suggestions made by Council members were incorporated in the design. Six of the miners came to Whitby to watch Mrs Sinclair, wife of the Council's Chairman, open it officially at the end of June.

It happened, then, that the park which had first been thought of the year before Queen Victoria was crowned, then proposed as a tribute to her long reign, was finally completed with a ceremony marking her grandson's Silver Jubilee.

Left, top:
The Jubilee Gate

Left, bottom:
Mrs Sinclair entering the park at the opening ceremony
Courtesy of The Whitby Gazette

Chapter 4.
The design of the park

Alderman Pannett had clear ideas about the kind of park he would like to see – a green and pleasant place where everyone, young and old, could relax well away from the noise and bustle of the streets and enjoy fresh air, flowers and bird song.

Quietness was evidently important to him; some music he could allow, but only the occasional concert, and he could accept that a charge might be made for it but only so long as the rest of the park stayed open to the public. He did not mention games. That may have been because the slopes are too steep for organised games or because he knew there were more suitable sites nearby.

We do not know which parks and gardens were his models. He had friends in Harrogate and evidently admired the sheltered gardens with their beautiful flower displays in the centre of the town contrasting with the open meadows of the Stray. He would have known the parks and gardens of London. Nearer home, Whitby's neighbours and rivals in the tourist business were creating new public gardens – for example, Saltburn had its Valley Gardens. Jack Binns, in his 'History of Scarborough', shows that their pleasure grounds increased from 50 acres to 350 acres between 1897 and 1933, and that Peasholm Park was under construction even as the Alderman was trying to persuade Whitby Council to take over the Chubb Hill Estate.

Right, top:

The Park: trees; grass; tranquillity

Right:

The rose pergola in Pannett Park

These contemporary parks and pleasure grounds have certain features in common.

Flower beds, where colour schemes changed each season, though a Victorian innovation, were very popular. Rose beds, trellises and arbours were almost always included in interwar gardens as were rockeries with alpine and other small, exotic plants and bulbs, often with waterfalls, pools and rills too. Indeed, water features were included wherever possible. Exotic species, which many nurseries were introducing to the market, were often used – azaleas, rhododendrons and primulas were especially popular. There was a tendency to plant many evergreen shrubs and trees among native, and introduced, deciduous trees to provide winter greenery and shelter.

Above:

The formal planting and the fountain at the lily pool

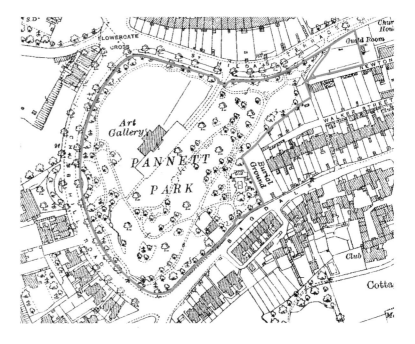

Right:

The park and its environs – 1928 OS map 4th edition
Ordnance Survey

The plans

Unfortunately Mr Brydon's plans have not survived.
The sources we have to rely on to build up a picture of
the original design are the Ordnance Survey maps of
1928 and the 1930s, a file of receipted bills paid by
the Trustees which luckily survives in the Museum
Library, reports in the Whitby Gazette and photographs
and postcards which have come to light. There is also
the physical evidence in the park today.

Though the park has the great advantage of a
sheltered and sunny aspect as it faces mainly south
and west, the steep slopes falling away from the
plateau alongside St Hilda's Terrace and running down
to busy roads on the boundaries, posed considerable
difficulties. Clearly, two features were 'givens'. At the
top of the hill there was the art gallery/museum, with
formal terraces in front, emphasising their importance,
which, it seems likely, the architects designed. And at
the bottom of the hill there was the Park Keeper's
Cottage with its outhouses and garden (see Chapter 3).

We do not know how much Mr Brydon changed the
contours, or indeed if he would have liked to make the
site even more dramatic. Some earth moving
was done but we can only guess where land was
levelled or slopes modified – to make the platform
for the lily pool and shelter and to create the Chubb
Hill rockery, for example. It is clear that Mr Brydon
concentrated his efforts on creating 'scenes' within
the park and making the most of views out of it to
Whitby Abbey, poised dramatically above the town.

Top:
Receipted bill for bulbs
from Kent & Brydon

Above:
A view of the abbey

Left:
The terraces in front of
the Art Gallery

The walks

The principal entrance to the park is from St Hilda's Terrace, where a drive leads to the art gallery and the museum. The way in from the lower end of the town is in Bagdale where a path with steps winds up past the lily pool. There are other ways in: the Jubilee Gates in the northwest corner; a gate near the junction of Bagdale and Chubb Hill Road; and another from Union Road. Originally this last entrance was closed with a door not a gate. In the early years the park was locked at night and everyone had to leave when the closing bell rang. Latterly, un-gated entrances mid-way up Chubb Hill Road and in St Hilda's Terrace were added.

The paths Mr Brydon laid out led the visitor round the park, taking advantage of the contours and winding up or down hill past all the attractive and colourful features as well as the quiet lawns. Sheltered seating bays were set at frequent intervals. Only one route led across the park – the path from the corner of Chubb Hill Road to St Hilda's Terrace.

The paths were, initially, finished with cinders, presumably on grounds of cost. They quickly succumbed to frost and rain and began to wash away. As early as 1933 the Whitby Gazette was complaining that *'to a person no longer active the negotiation of the 'brant'* [steep] *bits is fraught with terror'*. The Council was slow to act but, at last, in the winter of 1936/7 put in a more permanent surface. Erosion and slippage continued to cause problems, however.

Above right:

The entrance to the park looking towards St Hilda's Terrace

Right:

The view from the drive

The features

The classical portico at the entrance to the art gallery set above the formal terraces, with steps and flower beds, introduced a formal element to the park from the beginning. The early photographs show the flower beds and borders which we recognise today. Some of the embellishments, for instance the seats, the urns and tubs of flowers, the sundial on the lower terrace, have gone or been replaced. Some of the trees which framed the scene have been removed, others have grown, inevitably, much larger, but the design still pleases.

Rockeries, large and small, are also an enduring feature of this park. They proved a useful solution to design problems where slopes are very steep, as they are above the entrance from Union Road, and beside steps, such as those leading from the terraces towards Chubb Hill Road. The extensive rockery near the lower end of Chubb Hill was a major feature in the early years. The design included a waterfall and three pools *(see page 23)*. Unfortunately, there are no streams in the park.

Below:
This aerial photograph from the 1970s shows the aviary near St Hilda's Terrace

Above:
This sundial once stood below the art gallery

This area seems to have been rather boggy and Mr Brydon may have hoped to tap water running through the hill but, if so, the flow was uncertain and evidently failed, for the pools dried up though the rocks can still be seen. Local people remember the rockery as a temptingly wild place to play.

A more enduring and much loved feature was the lily pool with its fountain (latterly fed by a piped supply) and the shelter beside it. This pretty setting was planned as a convenient refuge for people at the lower end of the town. The designs have, or rather had, a decidedly 'Arts and Crafts' quality (still fashionable in the 1920/30s) though with a rather formal, contemporary arrangement of rockery plants and evergreens enhancing the paved terraces.

Top right:

The rockery beside Union Road (shown here in 2007) was later colonised by 'Bear's breeches' (*Acanthus mollis*)

Above:

The remains of the Chubb Hill rockery were replanted by the Friends of Pannett Park. This photo was taken in 2008

Right:

Visitors to the park enjoying the terraces and the aviary at the lily pool

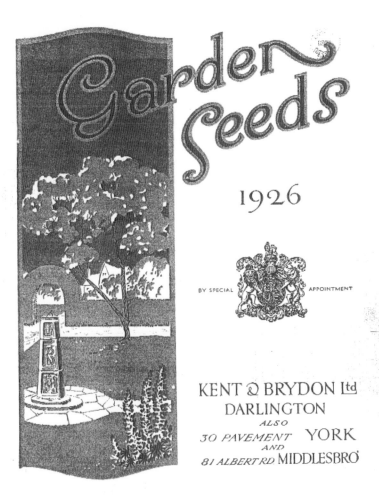

Garden Seeds

1926

BY SPECIAL APPOINTMENT

KENT ⊘ BRYDON ltd
DARLINGTON
ALSO
30 PAVEMENT YORK
AND
81 ALBERT RD MIDDLESBRO

Right:

One of Kent & Brydon
catalogues, found by
Fiona Green

The plants

The only certain information about the original
planting comes from the surviving receipts,
occasional reports in the Whitby Gazette and
catalogues from Kent and Brydon's Nursery which
give an idea of the very wide range of plants they
could supply. It seems that relatively few of the
donated specimens, mentioned in the previous
chapter, still survive. This could be because some,
the rhododendrons for example, would have
struggled on the neutral, fast draining soils of the
park. In other cases, over seventy years and more,
they have simply come to the end of their lives.

Apparently Mr Brydon made good use of the fruit
trees, shrubs and other trees which he inherited
from the former nurseries, though some were felled.
The Whitby Gazette reported that local boys had
made bird boxes from the wood under supervision.
People were used to the fruit trees for it seems they
had been allowed to walk through the nurseries
sometimes. So long as the trees were healthy and
not in the way of other projects there would be no
reason to be rid of them. For some years the Council
sold the fruit to raise money for maintenance. In a
good year it could fetch a useful sum. In other years

they were thwarted by bad harvests or because people simply took the fruit – *'a great temptation to younger boys and girls'*. In 1935 there were loud protests when many fruit trees were grubbed up. One writer complained bitterly that, looking from the art gallery, there was nothing to see *'but numerous chimney pots and slate roofs, hitherto mercifully hidden by the trees'*. It turned out that they had suffered an attack of honey fungus. Now only a couple of pear trees and an apple remain. There are, though, many flowering cherry trees in the park which may have been planted to replace the fruit trees' spring flower display as the Council had promised to plant *'similar trees'*. Unfortunately, after more than seventy years, several of them are reaching the end of their lives.

Evergreens abound both in the trees and the shrubs. The native species include Scots Pines set in groups; hollies, in considerable variety, planted throughout the park; and yews of which there are several well grown specimens in the lower part of the park though elsewhere they are pruned to shrub height. Monterrey Cypresses *(Cupressus macrocarpa)*, a popular tree in the 1930s, were used in several places; for example, they line the path west of the art gallery. As well as the hollies, *Euonymus japonicus* and two varieties of winter flowering Viburnum *(V. tinus and V.x bodnantense)*, all extremely vigorous shrubs, were planted in many of the borders, though it is not certain that these last species were Mr Brydon's choice or were introduced later. The Viburnums provided some winter colour which was otherwise lacking.

Right, top:
Cherry trees flowering
in 2009

Right, bottom:
A surviving pear tree
in bloom in 2009

Among the deciduous trees, apart from the cherries, a few old ash trees which must predate the park have survived as have some well-grown birch. Most of the long-lived trees which were planted in the first phase, varieties of oak and Scots Pines, for instance, thrive. The more exotic planting which seems to have been done in the 1930s includes some cotoneaster tree species and several groups of an uncommon *Cornus mas*, a type of dogwood which produces masses of tiny, golden flowers in March. A Maidenhair tree *(Ginkgo biloba)* is mentioned in early accounts but it is unlikely to be the one which grows in the park today as it looks too young. The surviving bills mention few items – unspecified oaks, two dozen *Berberis stenophylla* a well known prickly shrub with yellow flowers and 100 beech, presumably for a hedge. It is probable that Mr Brydon's nursery supplied most of the trees and shrubs and their cost was included, but not detailed, in his accounts.

Above:

The tiny flowers of Cornus mas

Top, right:

Cornus mas glowing in the afternoon light, 2009

Right:

Early photograph of a Yucca growing in the Park

Courtesy of the Ord family

Early descriptions of the plants in the park lay some stress on both the beauty of the spring blossom and the variety of bedding plants and bulbs. Two hundred dahlias were ordered in 1928; a delphinium border is mentioned later. Bulbs must have been a lovely sight in the spring. Between 1929 and 1931 some 4200 bulbs were ordered of which 3400 were tulips and the rest were narcissi, snowdrops and crocuses. In 1934 as the Parks Superintendant showed the Whitby Naturalists' Club round the park, he pointed out species from distant continents such as Yuccas *(Y. filimentosa and Y. gloriosa)*, New Zealand Flax *(Phormium tenax)*, Star of the Veldt *(Dimorphotheca aurantiaca)*, Swan River Daisies in two varieties *(Brachycomes)* and mentioned a bed of pink polyanthus roses which were a favourite variety of the then Prince of Wales.

In May 1935 the Gazette reported that in a *'recent spell of cold weather it was not surprising to find that a number of residents and holiday makers resorted to [the delightful pleasaunce of] Pannett Park rather than the exposed parts of the cliff and the pier… The vari-coloured blossoms on many of the trees, a profusion of wallflowers in bloom and the delightful variety of rock plants combine to produce an entrancing colourful display which has been much admired…'*.

Alderman Pannett would surely have been pleased.

Left:
The Park seen from the Art Gallery terraces. This undated photograph was taken in the 1950s or earlier

A Laburnum tree growing below the Art Gallery

Chapter 5.
The park matures

Whitby's population has grown since the park was created and many more people are likely to use it. The essential character of the park has not altered but, inevitably, there have been changes. Trees mature and die; others are planted. Some features could not be maintained; others have been introduced. The museum has been extended to house its growing collections and the whole building was re-roofed in 1987.

Changes in the park in the 1940s

The first changes were the inevitable consequence of the outbreak of War in 1939. The winter of 1940 was particularly cold and the Whitby Gazette again commented on the welcome shelter of the southern and western slopes – and complained of a lack of seats. Spare seats were brought in from the Sports Ground. Later that year the flower displays were evidently very fine but shortly afterwards the staff were authorised to grow root vegetables instead, no doubt as part of the 'Dig for Victory' campaign.

Above:
'Dig for Victory'
campaign poster
© IWM Images

Left:
Winter – the terraces
under snow

Behaviour in the park

The question of what is, or is not, acceptable behaviour in a park is as old as parks themselves. Much depends on what is generally agreed, at the time, to be properly respectful both of the park itself and of everyone's enjoyment of it. When this park was first opened it was common for people to stay on the paths rather than walk over the grass.

Park keepers and their staff would keep an eye open for anyone disturbing the peace or the flower beds. Pannett Park was shut at night and the Keeper, Mr Collier, *(page 17)* whose word counted, made sure that everyone left when he rang the closing bell. Nevertheless, the Whitby Gazette, even in the early days, reported occasional misdemeanours such as taking fruit *(page 33)* and when the park staff was reduced during the war the editor commented, rather crossly, that children and dogs were running about on the lawns.

Until 1974 Whitby Urban District Council employed a uniformed town policeman who patrolled the park among his other duties about the town. There was no climbing trees or scrumping for apples while he was about. Older people remember with affection Mr Les Stainthorpe who held this office for a time before he became curator of the Abbey. Later he was awarded the British Empire Medal and made an honorary citizen of Whitby for his services to the town.

There were, and still are, byelaws which list the things you may not do. Currently that means among other things, no dogs – except in Little Park – no cycling, and no anti-social behaviour. Vandalism is plainly intolerable and always has been though from time to time it has been a problem here too.

Right, top:

Les Stainthorpe
© Stainthorpe family

Right, bottom:

Enjoying the park,
21st century style!

Post-war additions: the 1950s

The post-war period saw several important changes. The first was the addition of the Kendall Memorial Room to the museum. Mr Hugh Percy Kendall was a man of many interests – history, antiquities and photography among others. He had proposed an extension to house the Museum Library in 1934 and when he died in 1937 the Literary and Philosophical Society and the Whitby Naturalists' Club (he was their Chairman) started a building fund. The war put a stop to the scheme and, given restrictions on building materials afterwards, it was not finished until 1950. It is on the north-eastern side of the original museum building and for many years it doubled as a lecture room.

Another addition was the Chapman Wing, named in honour of one of Whitby's most distinguished families who traced their connections with the town back to the 13th century. They were involved in shipping from the 18th century and, later, several of them played a prominent part in both local and national affairs. Dr Katherine Mary Chapman, a distinguished radiologist, followed Alderman Pannett's example of setting up a Trust to build the wing. Strictly speaking there are two wings, one either side of the original entrance to the museum. One houses a collection of model ships, the other contains material from Captain Cook's and the Scoresbys' voyages. These additions required some re-working of the ground outside to create the level platform north of the building which is now the car park.

Coronation celebrations in 1953

The foundation stone for the Chapman Wing was laid during the celebration of the Queen's Coronation on June 2nd 1953. The Urban District Council's ceremonies began in their offices in St Hilda's Terrace. Members then processed, through pouring rain, to the art gallery. Boy Scouts lined the route and, as the procession reached the flag pole outside the gallery, their leader broke out the Union Jack. Because the weather was so awful, members ventured outside only to lay the foundation stone and plant three commemorative trees. This, unfortunately, meant that the floral clock, designed to commemorate the occasion, was not turned on ceremonially; the key was handed over in the art gallery instead. The clock was the inspiration of the Whitby and District Chamber of Commerce who donated the mechanism and worked with the Parks Department on the design which took 20,000 red, white and blue plants that year. This cheerful addition to the park's attractions beside Chubb Hill Road was decorated afresh for several years until the hands were seriously damaged. In 1979 it was thought too expensive to repair so the face was grassed over but the mechanism was left in situ.

Left:

The library in the Kendall Room, opened in 1950

Above:

The floral clock in 1968 celebrated the bi-centenary of Captain Cook's voyage in the Endeavour

The aviary

The first structure by the lily pool was replaced with a concrete and fibre glass building near the Jubilee Gate donated by Mrs Kirby in 1967/8. People gave birds from time to time – parakeets and budgerigars for example – and for a short time a characterful peacock called Louis attracted attention. However there were serious concerns for the welfare of the birds at night and in bad weather. Interest in caged birds declined and age took its toll of the building. Then vandals attacked it and some birds died of fright. The decision to close it and find new homes for the remaining birds was finally taken in 1989. The building was demolished the next year and the area designated for children's play.

The weather station

The Literary and Philosophical Society had kept records of Whitby's weather from the 1860s. Instruments were moved about the town until 1906 when they were set up in Chubb Hill Gardens with Alderman Pannett's agreement. Following a break while the park was built, they were sited below the Art Gallery until they were collected into a 'weather station' near St Hilda's Terrace. The park keeper looked after it for some years until the Grammar School took over in the 1950s. Readings were sent every day to the Meteorological Office in London who published national data. Sunshine records particularly were used to promote holiday resorts. Students took it in turns, week about, to read the instruments morning and evening, throughout the year, on their way to and from school during term time. You had to climb a ladder to collect the sunshine records which was a hazardous business. The instrument, a Campbell Stokes Sunshine Recorder still in use, depends on a heavy glass ball sitting on top of a pole. At the old weather station this could be dislodged and was likely to hit you as it fell. Perhaps it is not surprising that vandals attacked this too and the station was relocated at the Grammar School (now the Community College) in 1966 where it still operates.

The cottage

By the late 1960s the old Park Keeper's Cottage (see Chapter 3) needed serious renovation. The Council decided that it would be cheaper to house the park keeper, at that time Mr Peter Wright, elsewhere and use the cottage as a garden store. However, it was difficult to keep it secure and in 1971 it was demolished and the land taken into the park.

Right:
The Park Keeper's Cottage, drawn by Albert Pile

The lily pool and the shelter

Sadly, the lily pool and shelter were frequently vandalised and defaced from the late 1960s onwards. In 1970 the Council considered filling in the pool but relatives of the donors, the Kirby family, protested that their gift should be kept intact and the Councillors changed their minds. The pool is still there but the fountain was removed. Vandals persisted in attacking the shelter and, in the end, repairs became so expensive that it was felt better to remove temptation. It was taken down, reluctantly, and only the terracing remains. The plants, of course, suffered too and this area became a very sorry sight indeed.

Management

The Urban District Council and the Literary and Philosophical Society found the 1928 arrangements for management and maintenance were not satisfactory after all. They went back to the High Court in 1948 and concluded a new agreement which, in essence, still stands. While each organisation is responsible for matters which are their sole concern, their common interests in the park, the art gallery and the buildings are determined by a Joint Management Committee composed of nine local authority members and six from the Society.

However, in 1974 with the reorganisation of local government, the Whitby Urban District Council was abolished. Some of its responsibilities were taken over by Whitby Town Council and the rest went to Scarborough Borough Council. The Town Council are still the owners and trustees of the park, the art gallery and the buildings and the arrangements between them and the Society continue as before. Scarborough Borough Council took over the management of the park.

Above left:
Graffiti and neglect at the lily pool and site of shelter, 2007

Above:
Lily pool looking east in 2008

Left:
The roof of the Art Gallery and Museum was replaced in 1987

Resources

Resources for parks and open spaces were steadily reduced everywhere in the country from the 1960s onwards as successive governments insisted that local authorities spent less money. Services such as housing and education are statutory duties but providing parks and open spaces is not, so these budgets were more severely cut. Staff numbers fell and there was less money for maintenance. Various other government decrees, such as compulsory competitive tendering for work in parks (1988), led to further financial constraints with the result that managers had to concentrate on essential, day-to-day maintenance. The upshot was that by the 1990s, throughout the country, many parks had become overgrown, untidy, and even unpleasant places, and no longer served the purposes for which they had been created originally.

Pannett Park suffered too, though not perhaps as seriously as some others. Since it is the only park in the town and Whitby depends very much on its visitors, it is important that it looks as pleasant and

attractive as possible. The lawns were kept tidy and flower beds survived though weeded less thoroughly than they had been. Some new trees were planted. However, there was not enough labour to do the more time consuming work of pruning shrubs and weeding difficult areas such as the rockeries. Plants such as sycamore, laburnum and ash, which readily seed themselves, invaded several areas. Vigorous shrubs grew bigger and bigger. The park began to look heavily overgrown and unkempt and in places rather threatening. During the day people walked through it, happily enough, on their way across the town as they had always done, took their children to the swings and came to the art gallery and museum.

Below:
A peaceful place in a busy world...

Right:
Some of the larger shrubs.

Photos taken in 2007

Interest in parks revives

Visitors, and locals too, continued to eat their picnic lunches or enjoy a rest in the park, sitting on the sunny benches in front of the art gallery or those which overlooked the rose beds below St Hilda's Terrace. At night, however, the park was increasingly vulnerable to vandalism and anti-social behaviour.

People soon realised what they were loosing as their parks declined and started to agitate for action. In 1984 English Heritage began to publish a Register of Historic Parks and Gardens which they completed in 1988. A House of Commons Inquiry into Town and Country Parks reported at the same time that action was imperative. Civic groups and Friends organisations sprang up to lobby for their much-loved parks. The National Heritage Memorial Fund, set up under the National Heritage Act 1980, and the Heritage Lottery Fund, founded in 1994, channelled money to projects for restoring important buildings and, at last, in 1996 the Lottery fund established an Urban Parks programme. This met with such demand (187 applications in 8 months) and such success that it continues today as the 'Parks for People' scheme.

A new era had begun.

Above left and left:
Terrace beds in 2008

Chapter 6.
New beginnings

In 2004 a substantial addition to the museum was opened. Built with the help of the Heritage Lottery Fund, it is a three storey extension to the west side of the original building which houses new exhibition and storage space, a lecture room, a café and offices for museum and Town Council staff.

The foundation stone was laid by the Marquis of Normanby, grandson of the Rev Marquis who performed the same function in 1931. The Literary and Philosophical Society can now mount temporary exhibitions and events. For example, after a fire on Fylingdales Moor exposed much Bronze Age rock-art, the society put together a project on archaeology and regeneration which included a major exhibition in 2007 and, at the same time, gave local sculptor, Viv Mousdell, the opportunity to demonstrate modern rock-art in the stone circle she laid out in the park. Such initiatives bring more people to the museum and, of course, into the park. Currently about 20,000 people visit the museum each year.

Above:
The latest extension to the Museum
© Roger Dalladay

Left:
Viv Mousdell's stone circle sculpture

Above:
Stone circle – detail
© Marcus Byron

The Friends of Pannett Park

The Friends of Pannett Park met first in July 2005 with the support of both Whitby Town Council and Scarborough Borough Council. The group brought together local people who wanted to see the park restored and properly cared for. The Whitby in Bloom group were among them. They have organised Whitby's entry to 'in Bloom' competitions with great success for many years. The Friends immediately set up weekly working parties to tackle the backlog of maintenance work under the guidance of Mr Tony Dominiak, the Parks Supervisor in Whitby and his staff. Shrubs were pruned, flower beds and rockeries weeded and new plants added which soon made a visible difference. The working parties continue their good work and many remark on how much more attractive the park looks these days.

One of the Friends' initial objectives was to restore the floral clock. They succeeded in a bid to the 'Your Heritage' Fund and, in August 2006, a new clock, in the same position as the 1953 original, was unveiled together with a Whitby timeline in the pavement below it. This very effectively gave notice that work was afoot to restore the park to everyone who went along Chubb Hill Road, now one of the busiest roads in the town.

However, the Friends' chief objective was to raise funds for major restoration in the park which was needed, for example to deal with ageing trees, deteriorating paths and steps and neglected features. Working under the guidance of Scarborough Borough Council staff and with the blessing of Whitby Town Council, the Friends applied for a grant through the 'Parks for People' Initiative. There is a great demand for these funds so applicants are asked to prepare a 'bid' showing in detail what they propose, why, and how much it will cost. It is a competitive and rigorous process.

Above:
Friends of Pannett
Park replanting on the
floral clock

Above right:
Friends of Pannett
Park logo

The rockeries flourish again thanks to the Friends

Two of the Friends with the contractor in April 2009

The Lottery bid

The story of the bid and the enormous effort that went into producing all the studies, background material, and plans which were needed is for another time. It took three years of hard, concentrated work, a great deal of volunteer input, various exhibitions and projects to involve the public and make the proposals clear, and the expert help of landscape consultants TGP Landscape Architects. Finally in January 2009 came the welcome news that the bid was successful. £1.4 million was awarded which, with additional contributions from the two Councils and other bodies, produced a total of nearly £2 million for the project. Following competitive tendering, John Hellens Contracts Ltd were appointed to carry out the main restoration contract in April 2009.

LOTTERY FUNDED

A park for the 21st century

The new plans are based on the premise that it is essential to respect Alderman Pannett's intention of providing a peaceful, green oasis in the heart of the town to serve as a pleasant retreat for visitors and townspeople alike. At the same time the park needs features which will attract people into the park and encourage them to come often. Exhibitions, workshops and working parties were set up to encourage local people to put forward their ideas on how this should be done. The restoration of the area round the lily pool was given high priority in the consultations. The fountain will be replaced, an open shelter built on the site of the old one and planting reflecting the original design introduced. Similarly the children's play area needed better equipment and a more enticing environment; here the proposals are developed from ideas which appealed to children who took part in a workshop. Some other features which will be introduced include a quiet

Commemorative Garden and 'gardens' within the park relating to major holdings in the museum such as the Jurassic fossils and Captain Cook's expeditions.

The major effort, however, will be to ensure that the park can be used easily by everyone – steps, gradients, surfaces and signs will all be improved. Visitors will need pleasant places to sit so new seats, and more of them, will be installed. Lawns, refurbished flower beds, the restored rockeries and the new 'gardens' must be well designed and maintained. Work on the trees and shrubs will aim to establish – or re-establish – more variety with less emphasis on evergreens and more colour and interest through the year as well as an age structure which will ensure that the park maintains its character through many decades to come. All this work will require many skills so the plan includes training schemes for volunteers and for staff.

Left:
Family fun at the museum: designing a new play area

Above:
Children enjoy the new play area shortly after its opening in August 2009
© Marcus Byron

The result of all this work will be that the Pannett Park, created in the 20th century with Alderman Pannett's and other donors' money, will continue to serve the same essential purposes in 21st century Whitby as all those good people originally intended.

Below:
Sections from Alderman Pannett's will

Bottom of page:
The Alderman's signature from the County School Record Book

15. I DEVISE my freehold land and premises known as the Chubb Hill property situate in the Township of Ruswarp in the County of York and containing between eight and nine acres and lying between St. Hilda's Terrace and Bagdale And also my freehold Pump Room Spa

to my Trustees In trust in the first place to dedicate to the public use a sufficient part of the said Chubb Hill property to widen the public road in front of St. Hilda's Terrace to a total width of sixty feet from fence to fence

the said Chubb Hill property Pump Room Spa and premises shall be held in trust for the inhabitants of Whitby as and for the purposes of a Public Park or Public Parks Recreation Grounds Gardens Pleasure Grounds Promenades and Public Walks and if deemed expedient by my Trustees as a site for the erection of the Public Museum or Building hereinafter mentioned the enjoyment thereof to be free and open to all the said inhabitants except that for not exceeding ten days in any calendar year musical performances or musical entertainments may take place the expense thereof (if any) to be defrayed the

(c) In or towards maintaining the same or any part or parts thereof as a Public Park or Public Parks Recreation Grounds Gardens Pleasure Grounds Promenades and Public Walks but not for the provision of games music or musical entertainments

(d) In or towards the erection on land so purchased or on the said Chubb Hill and Bagdale properties or any of them or the adaptation of existing buildings for the purpose of a Public Museum or Building for the reception and preservation of my water colour drawings works of art and objects of natural history and other things